Blend Hunt

Written by Kassi Gilmour

Illustrated by all-free-download.com

Practise the sounds

m   s   t   a   p

i   f   c   r

The Blend Hunt books are designed to help children practise blending new sounds within each set. Once each word is successfully blended, children search for the item that matches the words they have read on each page.

Practise tricky words

my   is   the

I   a

Blend Hunt

Set 1

Written by Kassi Gilmour

Illustrated by all-free-download.com

m a t

cat

sit

pat

c a p

f i t

r a t

Tam

Written By Kassi Gilmour   Illustrated by Eliza Burley

Practise the sounds

m s t a p

i f c r

Practise blending sounds

rat cat Tam pat

fat trap spat

Practise tricky words

my is the

I a

Tam

Set 1

Written By Kassi Gilmour   Illustrated by Eliza Burley

Tam is a cat.

Pat Tam.

The rat is fat.

Rat spat at the cat.

Cat traps the rat.

The rat taps.

Pat my cat.

Questions:

1. Who is Tam?
2. What does the rat do?
3. How does Tam respond?
4. Do you think Tam deserves a pat?

Trim Tam

Written and Illustrated By Kassi Gilmour

Practise the sounds

m s t a p
i f c r

Practise blending sounds

sit cat Tam pat

tip trim taps

Practise tricky words

my is the

I a

Trim Tam

Set 1

Written and Illustrated By Kassi Gilmour

Sit Tam.

Tam is my cat.

I trim Tam.

My cat taps the cam.

Pat my cat Tam.

Questions:

1. Why does Tam need a trim?
2. Where does all the trimmed fur go?
3. Why does Tam tap the camera?
4. Do you think Tam deserves a pat?

My Trip

Written By Kassi Gilmour
Images from Canva.com

37

Practise the sounds

m s t a p
i f c r

Practise blending sounds

Pam cat Tam sit

camp trip tram

Practise tricky words

my is the

I a

My Trip
Set 1

Written By Kassi Gilmour
Images from Canva.com

I am Pam.

I am at the tram.

Tam is my cat.

Tam is at the tram.

I sit.

My cat sits.

My trip.

I am at camp.

Tam is at camp.

Questions:

1. Who is Pam?

2. Where is she going?

3. Who does she take?

4. What do you think they will do at camp?

At the Ramp

Written By Kassi Gilmour
Images from Canva.com

Practise the sounds

m s t a p
i f c r

Practise blending sounds

at tap Sam pit

fit sips ramp

Practise tricky words

my is the

I a

At the Ramp
Set 1

Written By Kassi Gilmour
Images from Canva.com

The ramp.

I am Sam.

I am at the ramp.

I am at the pit.

Sam is fit.

Sam sips at the tap.

Sit at the ramp.

Questions:

1. Where is Sam?
2. What does he do at the skatepark?
3. Why does he need to be fit?
4. Have you tried skateboarding?

Camp

Written by Kassi Gilmour

Graphics from all-free-download.com and Canva.com

Practise the sounds

m s t a p
i f c r

Practise blending sounds

Sam cap cam sip
fit tap camp

Practise tricky words

my is the
I a

Camp

Set 1

Written by Kassi Gilmour

Graphics from all-free-download.com and Canva.com

I am Sam.

I am at camp.

My cap.

My cam.

The map at camp.

My trip.

Sam is fit.

Sam is at the tap.

I sit at the tap.

Sam sips.

Questions:

1. Where is Sam?
2. What does Sam do?
3. Why does he pack a cap and camera?
4. Have you been camping or on a hike?

www.ingramcontent.com/pod-product-compliance
Lightning Source LLC
Chambersburg PA
CBHW042131100526
44587CB00026B/4262